THE ORACLE OF TEARS

Mbuh Tennu Mbuh

Langaa Research & Publishing CIG
Mankon, Bamenda

Publisher:
Langaa RPCIG
Langaa Research & Publishing Common Initiative Group
P.O. Box 902 Mankon
Bamenda
North West Region
Cameroon
Langaagrp@gmail.com
www.langaa-rpcig.net

Distributed outside N. America by African Books Collective
orders@africanbookscollective.com
www.africanbookcollective.com

Distributed in N. America by Michigan State University Press
msupress@msu.edu
www.msupress.msu.edu

ISBN: 9956-578-27-4

For Ngum and Fonkeng,
Dearly Beloved
And
To the pioneer students
Of the minority literature class,
Tirdent Technical College,
Charleston SC,
Who
Saw a Tear
In my laughter

Table of Content

Author's Preface

A reviewer recently referred to one of the latest collections of Anglophone Cameroon poetry as one of 'odd' poems because of no 'thematic categorisation'. In identifying the collection as such, in a critique that is overwhelmingly positive, the description itself reflects the socio-political space of the creative task, and appears to suggest a certain formal comportment as of chaos in compilation – Jazz music may be the closest approximation to this analogy – that ironically respects the identified need to thematise the State of Cameroon as a schematic bundle of variegated strands of influence with no sub-heads: in other words, a perfect prototype for the troubled artist with no conscious blemishes that may result from, and into, boundary formations which inevitably lend themselves to respective ideological positions. Not that such organisation would have taken anything away from the subtle perceptiveness of the collection, but rather that it serves as a pointer to the fact that even the famous definition of poetry as 'powerful emotions recollected in tranquillity' is questionable, if not falsifying, and preys on our very understanding of the defiant nature of an emotion. When the artist allows consciousness to be the overall determinant of his or her vision toward psycho-emotional engagements (whether personal or communal), we risk losing sight of the fine thread of visionary unawareness that alone can suture the poles of socio-economic fact with political promise and expose the whitewashed spots of conscious representation.

If 'thematic categorisation' could seduce us into a needful dialogue with inscrutable authority and give hope to the betrayed plebe, then we may begin nurturing even implied reservation for its lack; only that the realism which such thematisation anticipates will fly in the face of a twisted, inconsistent, and overlapping communal evidence. The 'se porte bien' rhetoric which has been characteristic of our inverted state of social security leaves us all yawning at the end of the day because it is pampered and propagated by patriots who don't know the cost of a ballpoint pen or of a litre of kerosene, representative items on which the national enclaves place all hope for the future. And so, consequently, we find ourselves in a country with no credible roads (mainly because contacts are tendered, awarded, and executed in election campaign promises), and yet notorious for importing huge fuel-drinking 4-wheel runners. Such gross exhibition of national wealth baffles Brettonwoods technicians who still go on squeezing the national teats that have been squeezed almost dry by mutating SAP-type arrangements that eventually celebrate the peak of indebtedness as if it were an Olympic gold. Indeed, the tragedy of 'independence', evident in the sumptuousness of the recent *cinquantennaire* after which, today, babies cannot have their vaccines regularly because of a sudden shortage! But we know the sophisticated lie of bilateral fraternities and how it has been customised as a post-independence alibi against every evidence of failure: a rich man, no matter how conversant he is with the facts, can never speak objectively about the poor man's condition, since such an endeavour risks nullifying his own potentials and sense of difference. It is the same with urban-rural testimonies and denials about life in Canaan that have been replicated from Western hegemony in new hierarchies especially in African states. And when we then juxtapose constructed North-South imbalances with complicit top-bottom hegemonies of post-independence, it becomes clear that cushioning failure is a convenient pastime that validates the hypothesis of a failed state more than any other variable.

The Poet has been witness to all this globalising metamorphosis, which in Africa feeds on a pseudo and ill-conceived Neo-Liberal arrangement, and would love to record the externalised beauty if indeed it were genuine and sustainable. Then he too would chant the common song of Africa in miniature, an island of peace in a sea of turbulence, and become a genuine apologist for communal love and hope. But it is not so, has never been so, and his peace of mind remains an illusion that can never accommodate sleek, manipulative tendencies which bloom at press conferences and photo opportunities.

And how could it be otherwise then, in a country famous for cine and headline authenticity, incumbent infallibility, plebeian caricaturing, and lactational maturity on the international stage of who-says-what-and-why? We have been witnesses to a phenomenon of whitewashing our streets only on the eve of an august visit, thematised then as a fitfully salubrious show, after which our consciousness is once more conquered by staggering deprivation as budget controllers smear concrete walls with cement paste and call it decorative aesthetics; and 'paint' igneous rocks with black paint with streaks of grey in-between in order to ensure a perfect tally at the end of the financial year. And what can one then expect from this repetition of a pattern apart from a looted memory? And how else can this be represented except as a recurrent nightmare that can never adjust to the logic of a beautiful canvass? We could as well expect Pablo Picasso's *Guernica* to materialise into a romantic scene from a French pastoral! And our children become inheritors of contaminated knowledge, heavy and hollowed. We bequeath onto them the cursed seed of doom and they grow on it, cursed, if no new horizon emerges against the sordid skyline. But the greater curse is ours, and the humiliation, for onto us is granted the gift of knowledge of good and evil, of crime and punishment, and of the future and its endless horizons.

These views may be personal, but they are also representative. My generation has been a sacrificial one in Cameroon and anyone in this category who wishes to change their circumstance must of necessity 'belong' ideologically.

And to do so – say by objectifying wrong beyond Nazi mental grooming in Orwellian Big Brotherhood, institutionalising 'first province' arrogance and its attendant supremacist lie with stooping acolytes, or applying for a medal on national day beyond strategic Napoleonic nuances about toys and collective effort, and thereby rewarding mediocrity in most cases – is to deny one's self-dignity, sit on the fence, talk with water in your mouth, and rehearse a requiem song for a hypnotised humanity: all in the interest of a Far Right conspiracy that feeds on a Gaullist porridge. Yet, the poet who moans how 'across my home has grown the shadow of a cruel and senseless hand' also reminds us that hope is forever resurrected in the human heart, however mangled the horizon, since in the final analysis we may only be scared by the sound of our own wheels. This knowledge of possible doom and hope is the crucifix that the poet bears in every generation and in every culture, aligned with his wretched of the earth constituency, and remains the lonely guard in thin garb, metaphorically. In these our post-independence atmospheres in which every intellectual argument is appropriated to justify political wrong as goodwill, the risk for the poet's humiliation just as the temptation for him to file into the Crystal Palace is as great as the communal responsibility not to blink in favour of incumbent excesses. The complicity between the intellectual and the politician has been a unique and humiliating instance of Africa's insulting postcoloniality, and Cameroon has become an unfathomable case study. In this collusion, the shabby treatment of the artist, when compared with his counterpart elsewhere, is one of the best markers of our underdevelopment, as he forever remains on the fringes of society as the anti-Establishment outcast, and the typical prototype of Plato's suspicion against the same in the ideal Republic.

Yet, as the exiled Iranian poet, Marjane Satrapi, reminds us, the link between the love for country and criticism of same can only be hailed as an enabling instance of patriotism and hope, and not denied: 'I love my country so much', she insists, 'that's why I criticise it'. This collection, which mirrors such relationships by redefining them, has been in the making for over two decades partly due to roadblocks in the publishing industry in Cameroon. Few of the poems appeared in a collection that won first prize for the Bernard Fonlon Poetry competition and in *Black Voices*, South Carolina. Inevitably, however, I had to confront my Anglophoneness within amorphous Cameroon, in this collection: but not as the tribalised or ethnicised variable in the mosaic entity, but as a denunciation of this form of nebulous identification, which has been facilitated by surrendering *dimabola* apologists whose coffee estate roots, over the decades and through successive regimes, easily migrate against historical fact in denial of my roots, partly for the convenience of thirty rusted pieces of devalued CFA that often attend preferment. We have again been witnesses to such self-appointed patriots who define and defend Cameroon (with or without the *K* and *S* and *U* contextually), as a utopia created by God; and one without historical birthmarks of difference, even when it is evident that failure to recognise such difference for what it represents only breeds dangerous suspicion. And so circumventing *me* becomes an irresponsible endeavour in futility that is supposed to authenticate the patriotic credentials of such momentary drum-majors of the fatherland. Everyone is a patriot at any given moment, depending on certain terms and conditions. Indeed, even patriotism is deserved, and must be earned, failing which the rifts that inevitably develop on the national consciousness become the burden of an unforgiving posterity.

As we begin to explore the miracles of the twenty-first century, it is important to highlight the endemic reluctance that characterises Africa's forward movement as our own very undoing. The time for excuses is over, was over that February day when the gates of Victor Vorster opened and the Madiba, Nelson Mandela, walked out a free man with a heavy responsibility. The continental diplomacy of alibis was then dated and African leaders who had for so long hidden behind that screen started seeing themselves in the mirror as embodiments of the very horror they had constructed and sold at world conferences as unique only to Mr Pieter Willem Botha and his ancestors. Beyond the blame game and why it must be challenged today more than ever before, Africa's potentials continue to be grossly wasted and sentimentalised as a victim of Western-capitalist machinations. And this even when we see natural gas that burns up eternally (in Limbe for instance) while experts tell us that a pipeline can be constructed across the Sahara into Europe and that the resource will pay for its cost in less than a decade; when Europe now rallies itself to tap the African sun, care of Desertec consortium, in order to feed its ever growing energy needs and fend off Moscow's stranglehold on gas; when we see the abusive exploitation of timber without adequate ploughing back of benefits to the indigenes, and today depend on a UK NGO to check the abusive exportation of our wood; when we see the consequent inability to transform our forest into a veritable bargain chip in the economics of global warming even as Detroit alone emits more damaging gas than probably all of Africa put together; when we see the blind blundering into a globalised market where even 'futures' trading is unpredictable, partly because it is a market square in which the notion of 'a global village' thrives on such unpredictability and ensures President Obama or any future resident of 1600 Pennsylvania Avenue to be the glocal Chief or Fon for the next one thousand years at least; when we fail to read the signs that currently define the strategic muscling in the Gulf of Guinea whether for oil or territoriality or both as if we have absolute control over time and space and the human heart; when we see the devastating acceptance of Chinese junk in our homes because there is no notion of quality control, so that under the great, unblinking sun of the twenty-first century, Beijing is raping the African continent through an insidious form of a chopstick colonialism that blinds us all to its own composite iniquities; when we see the catch-up tactic of conceiving the African Union as an answer to the sins of the Organisation of African Unity, simply because Europe too evolved from the European Economic Union to the European Union: but we choose to ignore the ethnic solidification in Europe in such metamorphosis, while in Africa it is mostly Tripoli's agonising strategy to reinvent a hegemonic dialogue that should displace Washington if not through political leaders, then through their traditional auxiliaries, with Oilibya actually oiling the prostituting lips; and finally, when we see fundamentalist Christianity taking the continent hostage, thereby vindicating King Leopold II of Belgium, crucifying our ancestral consciousness on a new Golgotha along Wall Street and in the same breath transforming Jesus Christ into the universal ancestor.

No one can pretend to offer lasting solutions to the problems that plague Cameroon and Africa today. Yet, indicative tendencies can be offered in hopeful anticipation of the day when the Oracle will no more weep, but laugh and dance in celebration of our rediscovered manhood.

MTM, Yaounde, September 2010

Songs of a Man

The songs of a man
Broken at heart
Are the guardians of his love
In distant remembrances of first step.

And who shall say
I was happy, who knew
Not my heart beneath
My parting lips in the world?

For, the mirror of the world
Is a passing shadow over
Lucky heads in the sun,
And their mirth, like forgetful flames,
Conscripts the weeping heart
In waiting room of death.

Song for the Poet
(an excerpt, for bate besong)

I

Heart gushes of gall
In moments of a swooned
Apocalypse,
Fiddler in the desert;

His lonely heart tears spill
Over the visionary smiles, locked
In venal convulsions
Of the foetal hour.

And He
Shudders, enwebbed

In embryonic convulsions of
A Dele Giwa immolation rite on pavements
Of gore, blooming;

And, except for the
Undying ray, bowed
From his breast, and gathering
Fodder for burdensome prophecies
Of teeming days,
Trembles in recurrent deaths, the Poet.

And a limping prodigal
Dripping gutter, will deride:
'Is the barn worth saving
From fattened maggots
Of a faceless millennium?'

II

That is why,
Countrymen in adorned
Patriotisms,

But for the dark equatorial
Ray peeping
From the shadow of blood
In phoenix heartbeats
To bow dawn
Over the scorched hills
From sewage of kleptocratic
Wrong: we will continue feed the
Abattoirs of human dread after Biafra.

Did he not see, behind closed lids, the apocryphal
Apostle in whites,
Sharing dry bones to the hounds of the land, and
Preaching new deals

To an exhausted people, left and right?
And cried, He, iconoclastic stutter:
Anglo-dogs will never wail, never,
If boxed and sheeped, boxed and shipped, with
A ton of dry bones, across the Mungo-way...

That is why, beleaguered
Serfs in Kondengui khaki,
In your days of abundance,
Remember the Poet
In his dawn glimpses of sorrow

Since the rolling stones
That gather morning lilies
Know the easterly
Burden that is served the herded
Sinners in alleluia corridors.

Poets' Hemisphere

Whenever the Poet confesses his sins,
It is salvation for his people he wins:

They are gathered on the Fako, winged souls
Around a fountain of verse, smoking incense;

And I, shivering shoot on Ndamnyeh[1] ledge,
Crawl up, in painful fear, up the raggéd edge

For palpitating ritual at initiation,
On wordly canvass of salvation.

---

[1] my ancestral home

Resolution

The river in me flows
in circles: concentric turmoil
of the laugh, of the heartache,
seeking estuary for bled sleep.

So I'll confess myself
first to my soul: and be happy,

then to the sneezy world,
and be crucified.

Hosannas on a Birthday

O Henry,
O my King
(Murder in the Cathedral)

I

Come, let us chant hosannas
to the Prophet, our
shepherd; let us
chant the sweetened harmonies
and proclaim the metaphysics
of quadrupled years
in unparalleled gospelling,
prophesied from the paint-smelling
rotunda of a national sweat.

These are the marks
of an era that
ridicule History's inscrutable
face in a psalm of faith.
What voice – since

we hearken to every voice,
acquiescing – declaims the Spartan
behind vulnerable flesh,
the Saint with a human heart?

II

Many voices there are
that will sing out of tune,
in unison, if you only listen beyond
the hollow din of your
anniversary; hear the side-lined voices
so distanced from your communion,
unable to sing and live
for a swelling god.

These are the voices that
show a generation
from underground playgrounds
or barbed wire zoos
pavlovering the electrocuting *bikutsi*;
pampered by lead-singers who stand
on the running-boards of the Great
Ideology, shackled vocalists in
hosanna dens.

III

The mind-sick we slew to forge this birth,
fixed their *mbaghelem* skulls on
banner-pegs to scare off
prey-things, are still living.

We proclaimed a dawn,
vowed from the whitewashed podium
in dominical veneration,

but we should see another dawn
from a cyclone of darkness —
except we still want to
sheep the gangway of
the Elysee's universe,
into astral hallucinations of a
cobbled dream.

When the Vultures Swoop

Tertiary truths we are lured
To swallow, panting for milk
Behind the shearers of our calf.

With sealed deals from trans-continental
Deal-shops of a Wall Street dilemma,
We are coyed to purchase
The chaff and sweat on the shoot
That is chaff and grain in one,
Watching America grow.

The intelligentsia will offer
No light, bugged in the shimmering halls
Of our intellectual dome, cowed into seat
By the pistons of the feathered ogre.

Therefore, the seeds that
Shall fall from the shoot; the seeds
That still feed on the blot
Of common knowledge, shall
Line the contours of this petering hilliness
And sway with their lanky shadows astray,
Languishing behind tertiary dusk-screens,
And loving America for American aid.

They shall sway to the beats of a borrowed
Liturgy, when the vultures shall swoop
At dusk, over scratched labyrinths in fovea dungeons,
To peck at the bones on smoking hills
After the last waltz of blood, to find
Only the chaff that was grain.

If Only You Knew

You mould my Golgotha
and trail my steps
for ocular hopes
after the lightning

because I seek valley ways,
firming flesh
against the tides of schemed fear
before the thunder crackle.

You shape my crucifix
and plant it on moulded mountaintop
as testimony against my sainthood;
rallying adversaries
to creep shadow ways
with infra lens

against my bleeding heart
when I too moan
like a man falling.

I see you groom a smile too
and rehearse jovial tactics
for the moment of hands-shaking
along the corridor
or at *Alice's*, calling

me pal and bro and stuff,
moulding my Golgotha:

Oh! How I weep for you,
sweating so much for me…

After Reading a Book

This glued and stained volume of paperback,
through finger-feels of a desperate hand
and under lust of my watery lamps,
shall again out-live
my straddling stay
of breath, of love, of hate;
and shelved, undusted,
shall of curious generations always tell
to searchers of aftertime
on the collective voyage,
how the days came
and the years went
and the seasons re-formed,
and the great collective endeavour
remained peripheral effort
on the final point of the last page.

Burden

Accumulated tons of
black divinities
hang over the heart-way
in marshalled shadows of
black paternosters.

And I watch the crowding steps ahead

and take my lone step
for the shrineway of
told days, making step
from sprinkled pattern of Mungo dust.

From the pinnacle of
the Anglophone Diaspora,
we shall save the day
with song for Juliette's[1]
preterminal wag of tongue.

Phoenix Song

The changing cycle of my life
Forms like an engraved brow,
At noon.

And in fierce winds
Push the land of my dreams
Into phantasies of brimstones.

And I wake
And cough ash,
The sputum of my convulsed cycle.

B'lues Feeling, Ngoaekele

I feel bad
giving myself away,
so bad
giving my life away,

---

[1] One of six victims shot by the police during the launching of the Social Democratic
Front (SDF) in Cameroon on May 26, 1990

here, on path of stone
lined up in my brains
like a crooked landmark,
crushing:

It is also love
that I crave,
letting my life away
to be used and twisted and smashed,
offering my soul away:

It is the pain too
that I court, hoping
for love in pain
with broken nails
and scaly palms
and ever-furrowed brow,
living the pain of love.

Lost
(for ernestine)

I
Searching for myself
Through midnight streets
Of insanity, moaning;

Grabbing straw-tips
For safety belts
Across chasms of doubt;

Lean days paint
Leaner shadows that stalk
The landscape of my soul

As I stumble on fringe of this palmed knoll:

Recollections crowd my head
As visions plague my view –
Of luring mermaids
With cat-paws-in-cortex; of chanting crowds
In ballrooms, denouncing my awkward pride
Over the common things
Of happy bosoms in rhapsody...

But every heart its secrets
Must nurse and garner,
Let the world roar mad in defiance.

II
Every rendezvous
Of my languorous day
Bears a bleeding crucifix,
And sears the heart like bellows'd steel
After the vacant hour of weakness.

Lubricants on scars
Unveil the weakness of flesh
In successive moments of surrender.

III
Isn't it a loud whisper
That men like statesmen,
Ever great in fronting their dailies
Also find their inner wears
Littered in tabloid phrases
Of a paparazzo's vagrant lust?

No secret is theirs as desired,
Caged in their hearts of eminence,

Because from their Nixon-podiums,
The public eye penetrates
Their steeled plates of heart, O Lewinski!

Man rises on the dignity of his faith
But his fame is forever snared
On slippery earth of civic scrutiny.

IV

But it is the love of my dream that I can't find here,
And now that my heart sizzles over happy flames,
Raging in tongues of vengeful glee,
I retreat, oh I must, in tears.

Almost pagan to my faith too,
I find no hope on this knoll,
No friend to guard my soul,
And no horizon to charm my heart.

All my faith is incarcerated
In long, fruitless endeavour,
As searchlights of wagging tongues
Pick out my heels over curb and gutter,
And no secret is mine – anymore –
When I slip and stumble and fall,
Searching for myself.

Sacrifice of Myself

Standing on the crowded highway
Of weighing isolation:
Kilometres of fancy coil the horizon
And rip my wondering mind
From this seven-hilled vortex,
On pilgrimage.

A thirsty mouth is a gaping cave
Even for drops from Calvary's sponge;
And the eye of Vision never blinks
Through confusions of mudded canvass
When even cripples itch at race-point
To touch the shrine-stone in redemptive bath.

I have made these observations before,
Ludicrous at times, to a paltry people
Minting gold on the sheets of God.

The nerve centre in every man, gathered in little loves and
hates,
Awaits the terrible hour of passion
Acknowledged at the point of silence.

Once in a long while, I saw the smiling day
Offer a rose into my desperate palms,
Its lavender to soothe a scaly memory on stranded pilgrimage:

I had then embraced the inflamed day,
Conquered the trembling within walls of silence,
And hailed the world in an instance of harmony
And pardoned too the hooded Philistines, daggers-drawn,
Of my dreaded kin, and my kin's dread.

II
The ways of man are not those of God,
But, in the end, they reveal His abode
In variegated presence of arched repentance across the River.
The way forward is actually
Backwards, retraced year after year
Across deserts of speeches, and of promises at rally time,
Before salutations of the conceived dawn.

My lowly cradle in Thunderland
Had fathomed beauties at peak point of desire
In soft, rainbow strokes of water and oil –
Smiling faces of a happy mind
In evergreen, sunny land, sucking nectar
In bee-horn and lulling the wrangling world
In a buzzing bough of olives and Nkoh frenzy.

Jehovah's witnesses shall surely remember
My hesitant trudge
On the rungs of life, torn in myself,
Unable to kiss the hackneyed God
Remoulded into multi-faced simpleton from Bethlehem,
In vocals of congregational condescension,
And, at last, witness at midnight ritual of Tekoh.[2]

III
And now for sacrifice of myself,
Forgetting the fears and the chats, the laughs and the kisses,
And the honours and the medals
With ribbons fashioned for faxed loves,
To remember only myself in homage,
Incarnated from history's contingencies, I,
And burdened with the Mungo's miscoloured arc!

I am the oracle of the shrine

Watching tribulation of banquet halls,
Swelling under froths of popped dreams;

I am the oracle, the word in the gourd,
The wine, the goat, and the cam wood,
Ancestral balm over thatched lintels;

---

[2] Family God

I am the oracle, to body forth
The scholar-heart in gilded robe,
And dare tongue-twisters on popular podiums.

I will be your Daniel, firmed from Kondengui chambers;
I will clog the paws of raging fury,
I will hack its mane of spiked fur,
I, your Daniel, in the lion's own den.
I will groom your multitude with Tcholliré grain
I will douse five loaves for five million Anglo-mouths,
And with Tole wine in fungused skins,
Consecrate the marriage of Water and Fire
Here besides the doubtful Mungo...
I am the lamb in Sikh dens, firmed in torture, laughed at by
the twisted decades
And the Anglo boot-licker:

Stoop into this shrine and have your wine and bread
And a bed for your woes and dreams,
For I disdain the weeping loungers of eternal grudge.

Come in even against the jingling charms of your humpy
lords,
Planting biblical Iscariots in every home:
I will give you bread and wine and dreams,
To herald the day of sails.

My feelers smell a new day and age
Over riddled dust of planted fears:
But I have saddled my pilgrimage
For victory
On altar of your tears.

Come then, come and grab your tormented dream.

To Our Hon. MPs on Their Last Extra-Ordinary[3]

And now, this sudden hands-linking
Across the gulfs of the decades
Ferrying the decaded typhoid of
Legitimate ire
Into shores of amorphous impotence;
And the sleek tongue-coating, speeching
Charities in prescribed tons at eye's blink,
In this hour of impotence.

In unholy gush of tears,
It chains Moslem in mid beads, to
Hoarsely Christian, still wriggling
On shell of divine land;
Coats the sniper's rationed balls
Against French helmets for the vague incumbent,
When in their mass or alien catacombs
They now fear nothing,
And desire no handcuffs of living fear.

And I declare:
The Present is what concerns us;
Should concern us now, with faithful trial of the Past,
That the dawn of this turbulent dusk shall feed on
The refracted interludes of the House's humours
Canonized for distant seasons of sunny green.

But only smells of fetid buds
Attend to the inquiring heart
From the late roars,
When fruitful blame is gagged
And love served in frantic spoonfuls, blinking.

---

[3] The last session of the one-party Parliament in Cameroon

What then in aftermaths
Of guilty pledges,
Fiddled for human memory?

Bred chaos shall still span
The face of our garden in selfish gests
And in the hurricane, fan singular
Blooms for sighs of colossal deprecation;

And our cemeteries shall daily grow
And vague smells of freshly cut roses
Spread into virgin decades
And cut the plate of memory with a sudden sob.

For when the Law is raped by senile
Charlatans of macabre pre-empting,
I remark again, and mark me for clemencies:
A hundred millimetres of mis-trek for the People's throes
Is a century's retreat for their woes.

Ally

I know your embrace
of thorns
and your smile
with spikes,
tearing hopes and visions;

but still cannot hate myself
for padding your way
to urge you toward your trophy,
over me.

I share in your turmoil

and watch you dance
in your moment of supremacy
when I oil your path
making you hard like a vice
against my willing fingers
when I massage your will.

So dance on, dance
like the strongman of your heart
and dance the groomed dance
of your dream...

History Makers

The slow grinding of his teeth,
Seeping the doses of his teen faith,
Inflates the sentry's baton-arm, rising
And falling, to cut flesh, here and there,
On reddened cobblestone of one thousand and three.[4]

And the spiked boots-in-*kiwi*,
Grind prostrated bosoms on cobble ways;
And red cotton fold from Eve's sacred cave
Reminds no one of our Moon's sinking hour
On frontier spot of unreprieved memory.

And shaken pedagogues
Abandon the weary place in oath
After their last step of patience,
And drag their soiled robes, for the Sun.

And who shall dare swear allegiance
To History, from complacent memories

---

[4] The Amphitheatre 1003, University of Yaoundé I.

Of breeded fear in lower chambers
From a nation's brain garden?

I Still Hear the Vulture

Our cultured jargon has finally
Betrayed our stride of manhood,
And failed the heavy hearts
That longed for assurances
In besieged vineyards,
Shadowed by a vulture's wing.

Can a string of soft, empty words
Stitch this gash of guilt
Which for fifty years has been ripped
By the painted lips that lip
The brush, whiting the pulmonary way?

Can the cord hold, when
Even this time last year
We sang in out-cries round the circled ways
For masturbations in gardened Jerusalem?

After these lips out of Gethsemane
Lipping a hundred seasons of thorny awe
In jingled catechisms
And now crouching the tiered House
With glossy smiles over dark ridges
And querying the People, *'Are we the ones...?'*

What is this that we await
In this lapse of our new incarnation
That I can't see nor imagine without
A shiver, wrapped in blood-soaked sheets
For a black, wet morning

This time next year?

What if it is the French vulture
Beaking a fading tricolour,
Beating the harmattan air,
And seeding the withered garden
In time-clocked obituaries
From her Eiffelian heights?

October 23, 1992

They seemed (because
with toupees of dark cream
from the nocturnal census
in bacchic baptism,
harvesting their own nettles
from the common tear-pool),
not Apollyon notifiers
in Supreme Court verdict
of the harlequin epilogue.

But vision of the slaughtered foetus
in hypertensive *essamba*-éclat
outside, along the whitened pavements:
they too had received their dose
of the *francaemiac* porridge
the night before.

Then undeclared national dirge
by the bereaved of the Nation

because oxygenating
Anglophone breathe over the parched fields
is Judased across the Mungo
for thirty inches of Che

Ngwa Ghandhi's tomb
whose laughter the day before
was fecund riddle
for the watchers of the land, in Tekumbeng.

How then should my Anglo-dove
roost, beaking olive bough for abounding eras,
since our balding breed from the French baby-sitter,
acknowledges yet a millennial repast in mortal chunks
of a nation's corpse in fetid bloom?

Our Exiles

They have reigned on favours
In warm, foreign lands, and vowed
To redeem the festering land's flavours
At triumphal return on Judgement Day.

But the farthest land from heart is Home
Where, drenched under the sinking roof,
They also wedge the falling dome
With evening lore of yore

Because not every Exile
I know, seeks the road.

Voice of the Anglophone Universe
(*for simon munzu*)

I
Your inscrutable toes breed light
at enclaved spots
of the stand-by hour, Munzu:

and the world observes from sandy banks
your offered breast
over the Mungo Calvary;

and heaves the paradisal sigh
of acknowledgement.

II
Heraldic umpire at parturition,
mangering the leprosed hearts
against Nebuchadnezzar's clansmen
in ashes: staff to limping sages
for Mungo seasons of plenty.

Anglo-Simon, wielding the nibbing sword
forged in mooted arena
of ancestral word-craft:

the hawkish tommy-rot from Etoudi
fissures, dripping fear, only tickles
(as with numbed fingers of their carbolic
vision) the salamander coating
of your estranged faith,
hammered in tortoise caverns
and flaming atop the Fako, Godward.

III
True, opiate utterances still couch
the leeway of doom
in *ganja* drills of a macabre prophecy...

Yet, weave your atoms of faith
for foot rug at Jerusalem's gate;
fashion the hand-chain of brotherhood, epicentral Voice,
and dove balms of smile against the tinkered hour of fear

for if fame from pain did grow,
then glory through pride must flow.

My Noontide Fading Blues

The ideal, very often, as for martyrs,
Is the burden of bridge-builders.
But in these barren halls of woe
That no grain of love can sow;
These barren caves, like stalags
To Freshman and Don in thin rags:
My eager steps have daily followed
A dream, slain in acres unploughed.

For I, not aware of my exile,
Have lobbied for redemption
From long cyanide seasons across the verbal chasm;

But from my boastful peaks of inconsistency
And riverbeds of misery,
Briars have embraced my lusty heart
With thorny crown as I leap across the Mungo trench.

What merry song then in my pricked breast
When showers of horror confound my rainbows?
For, no hymnal can lift this Fako off my heart
And give me reason not to doubt, though angels
With celestial chorus plait my hammock strait:

Every man has his Achilles-heel
And knows, where courage is drained
In supreme moment of watchlessness;

Where a flippant blade of grass
Defies chest plates and skull masks

Of balloon rituals along the musketeered stretches;

When Beauty's glory surrenders
To the hour of conquest
In a second of watchless vanity;

When deficient common sense
Betrays classroom ideals
In sickly mornings of incomprehension;

When the heavy purse
Harbours the manacles of slavery
After epicurean dawns of prodigal valentines;

When even knowledge of God
Is cassocked in fornicated memories
On the misty path of glory...

So then, my tearless farewell to the grey hill, palmed
In songs of pigmy dreams, if my heart's too full of me,
For the blues fades and dies to rise no more before sunrise.

On the Path of Glory

Those who plot my downfall
And pour libation in midnight rehearsals,
Have instead nourished the beast in me,
Alert to earthly danger, and in outer space too.

Those who in Agwoturumbe séances
Divine my punctured heart, deserted
On the doorstep of material benevolence,
Have at last mended my heartplates of manhood.

For all the knock-kneed schemers

Against my stride of aprodigal dreams,
No harlequin on jingling toes
Scares my resolute heart over murky streams.

Jesus alone possessed a heart of pity
For those whose pity nailed his love on the terrible tree:
He loved them and pitied them too much,
Who for him brewed vinegar in sponge-drams.

Alas then, my loyal heart, *en route*,
Ace migrant over coerced brotherhoods:
Flag my path on thunder hooves
And nurse the Child of my prayer, O God.

Flesh may break on Sisyphean heights
But anticipation of Parnassian visages
Fuels the ambushed heart through mystery cycles,
Feeding the soul.

Anniversary Dirge

Take my wreath of white, tears-bloomed;
Take my petals of white, you
Of the weeping fold in black *kabas* and *jumpas*,
Because the memory we hold, like a foetal hope,
Is the bloom in our veins, after thirteen moons,
Yeasting our dawn-led steps.

Else, what fractured memory can they banner
In balance sheet of our dreams-in-statehood,
Now exposed to the ridicule of charity nations,
Black and white, saint and mercenary?

Else, what have they in store, profit-made,
That bidders may swim our shores with cupped hands,

Since our barns, like fairy caverns,
Have only fed their Ali Baba pouches across the Suez?

Crippled of heart, crippled at heart,
They have limped in static endeavour of Machiavellian
tutelage,
And shown sweat beads of death at world conferences
To the ever sneering world because

They, our frenzied Mvolyean drop-outs
And coffee estate pensioners,
Still wallow the waste in dubious manhood
Before the great Anglophilic dawn.

So take my wreath of white, mourners
Under empty Fako rock, and ebb back the welling tears
Which only blur vision in bondage,
Over the Mungo pass-way.

What Vision do we Await?
(for willie m.)

What vision, like bats, do we await
In nebulous climates of clerkly Samaritans,
When carbuncular fingers infest
The breeding seeds of the anointed ray?

We saw the Eastern albatross
Swing across the Western plane at dusk,
And hovered over straw dreams
In sodden nights of annunciation;
And thought at last, Kondengui havens
Should vomit the intestinal rot of hardened conscience,
The agony of smeared dreams
On banks of a Mungo monsoon with fresh rays.

So what vision for us, you in oyez circles,
Sucking your little minutes of intimate loneliness,

Since in this den of seven cactus cones
The hearts of men, in need of vital memory,
Reminisce only hymnal four-four-four
Over the fantasy Eden of stalking shadows?

Mbeboh B'lues, After a Whooping Spell

I

The paths we cross, weak-limbed,
and re-cross in circles of madness
and bearing responsibility
like the David of a people, shouldering Golgotha
in long, clothed strides,

lead to God, whose multi-presence
is a garbed memory in meditation.

In cold counterfeiting dawns
the heart may grow fungi
and remembered hope entombed in stone halls of a palmed
lee-way;
or embrace the world's icy smile
from wooden faces
at crossroads: but whispering voice of this sepulchre,
where lately he preached,
holding a ray, beckons.

II

Like eaves of gold
glinting through ashes of rain charms,
the heart in penance glows

over neophyte messiahs, breeding
nightmares at noon.

Every man his God should choose
and learn to love.

This smile then chronicles the gardenings of absence,
fertilized residue of missing time
and rebirths the pampered heart
in embrace, like filings to the lodestone.

The Pinnacle of Gloom
(evening)

From the pinnacle of my gloom
I feel contours of smile
Recoil into gathering dusk
Like the shadows of doom
Sheltering the cropped head
Of my Valentine fount.

Horoscopes never predict death,
But the life they augur
May be wrapped in candled white
Dripping the tears of fixation
From the hinges of memory.

I have courted the rose too far
And embraced the thorn too deep,
Shattered by the pangs
Of an unfulfilled memory.

Horoscopes don't predict death
Because guilty brains, drilled
In word craft, may pause in mid-sob

And catch the world in a passing wit.

Let me gather my gloom now
Into the addendum of the silent hour;
Let me recall my heaps of fairy roses
As cushion for the mausoleum to rest,
Before the rippling words of the pagan crowd.

I Defy!

Who says I be dumb
And clip my lips
And watch the haranguing concert
Enacted by puppets of a nightmare?

Who prays I be sightless too,
When certain visions crumble
In colossal resurrection of evil
From particles of a dream that failed at dawn?

It is my soul that I worship, unblinking
In vision of ever new day.

This nib that I consecrate then,
Dipped in the restive blood of my woes,
Will trace thunder
Along path of rainbow;

And covenant the hushed voices
At summits of blotched visions.

Rainbow seasons alleviate
Hump-backed manacles;
And alleluia tongues in breadless homes
Curse God's benevolence in Canaan:

29

I defy then, phrase-masters
Bred as valet for Gestapo chambers,
Speeching crowded arenas.

I defy gold-seekers' wit,
Benched in clapping fit
Of a Glass Palace writ.

I defy the misery of fence-sitters here
Who sing of woes untold every year
And vie not beyond boundary of fear.

Let my faith my shield be in lease,
During thorny weathers of hydra kisses

For in defiant submission of sacrifice, Lord,
Thy will be crusaded against the spiteful horde.

Fate

I

The heart that must Beauty
Have, shall for Beauty die.

Shimmery horizons do I crave, knowing my end:
They urge my step, rising sun after setting moon,
And I turn away from the common sidewalk,
My eyes fixed on the skyline, ever receding;

And thinking, the surest way
To fall out of friendship
Is to fall in love
On beaten tracks.

And the Mendong sunset says,
I am your charm, your fate,
Seek me and know thy end.

II

Distant ridges court my meditative step
With milk and honey,
Bouquets of love, away from a land of sand.

The crunch of the day
Scatters seeds of fear
Over my tilled fields;
But by dusk time,
I see the wand, forged with the stars,
That will clear the fog
For my horizon to bloom.

III

Conspiracies against the migrating heart,
Feed desire and restrain the eager step;

It is my soul that the world sweats after,
But my faith is not of the world's, in congregation,

Even when my day is spent in glosses
And my lonely night in entrapped curses.

Over the ridges of my soul
Linking the banks of my desire,
I have invented the dream of my life
To lead me across the boundaries of fear
To the miracle of the glimmering frontier.

Tethered

I

Let me break, let me break away now, from
The dry tongues of this dry flame.
Who will break with me,
Now that it is near-time for baptismal vows?

The urges of the place restrain my soul,
Cleave my blistered feet to its slime.
The urge to run pains the feet, slashed feet
That no longer feel the earth where they stand,
Shackled onto this forsaken place
Of forsaken talk, by the sores of contact.

I must rush off with my soul, rush off
From myself, before immersion, at dusk;
Forsake my feet if they choose, without me, to stay.

I must die away from this flame
Licking the surface of my soul,
Now that the cord, with me in accord, snaps.

II

So I'll break off, far, far from here,
From the close-touch flavour of this stew
Vomiting the stewed flesh of sacrifice.
It bubbles on the fire-stones of doom,
Buried in the fore-house with blood paste.
My bowels that bubble in rage
Against the offered dish, urge
My soul away from me, away in flight:
And I feel faint, so faint I can't wait
To die the death of my crusade.

III

Let me fly away then,
In accord with myself in desire, flight-ward;
Let me fly the broken wings of my spleen;
Let me flap across the unformed lanes of my soul
And scan the tryst within my hungry soul
That guards the last juice-drops for its parched sail.

Then I should find a peace, like the shelled tortoise,
With myself, alone in myself, beyond dusk.

Then I should find a pad for my stance,
Unrestrained by the faggot-warmth of this
Patronized talk, before baptism ...

For so my sight from such stiff and dry ploys,
Seeks for pain that hurts the sight, uncoated;
Feels for knocks that hit with blunt anger in recompense,
And in amends, wipe away the tears.

So my soul in this stubborn feat
May still live for the days that keep a promise,
Days that launch a ray from above the Fako on gilded hoofs,
Dead to the chaotic lure of this re-fuelled flame,
Dead, always dying from this whirlpool of peace.

IV

But ah! No one wishes to break with me,
Entwined in contagious smiles, from their soft plush;
Nobody smells, like I do, the raw flesh
In this sharp evening wind, breeding smiles, official nuisance.
So you stay, you stay brothers, for the patronized
Speeches of doctrine before the sprinkle, wishing it were true,
The prophesy on the dry bed of mud, at dusk.

Perhaps the air I smell is of a different world, uncreated;
Perhaps the day too is of a different time, unstated
When for all this, as you are wont to stay,
I sacrifice for only the short visions of extending time,
While you wait, waiting like waiters of death,
For the sun from the East, at dusk:
Let me embrace my death, then.
But we are one, indivisibly so beyond knowledge,
And it my impatience to stay and toast and hum and bow
For the vacant show, that makes me weep in flight.

After Me
(in bed)

Like a sack of moistless mud
Stretched on the white-spread bed,
Dripping candle at four points,
And the Scriptures over breast;

Like unchanging chameleons
Conceding victory after the race,
The choristers in tuned, balm voices,
Wooing the starry plane:

But like me after me, venturing
Into unknown cycles,
The stretched lump shall be forgotten
By next dawn, beneath six feet,

And fattened thoughts of me after me
Shall re-visit crowds at dirge rituals
And tales of me after me, from bright heads,
Shared to highway gangs, bidding for relics.

When to Die

I'll dance now on your gravid lips of aroma,
And in the nakedness of my ecstasy,
Acknowledge the cycles of the moon, planted in your bosom.

I'll flutter on the lilies in your eyes,
And drink the nectars of honeyed joy,
And anticipate the day of manna over toil.

I'll erect your shrine in *bijou* fronds
And knit your skirt in fibre waves,
And make ritual steps from rhythm of your throat.

Rhythmic drums revive the rooted feet in circles,
Like your steps in *rumba* now teach me how to die.

Innuendoes of Love
(for befi, on stage)

You stretch your soul on a dangling string of verse
With infant desire and strive, peering the vapoured lens;

You trace breeding labours in uncertain patterns
Over certain meadow of your bosom, yeast of dawn;

You catch your thoughts like shadows in flight,
In the flying mystery of your mooted heart in labour;

You gather your momentous hours, day by day,
For fecund discharge of song at ritual of cleansing;

But scanning the sky for the joyous skylark,
You moan at convulsed abortions of astral dreams,

And survey the inundated sheet of earth
Through kaleidoscopic lens of your battling soul

Because your totem, earth-blanched, is the sea-blue sky,
And you weep over man's endeavour not to die.

Let your bleeding soul then be your Justice
Against the stony hearts of turmoil, at armistice:

Then the skylark shall again rise from your throat
And flap a path, like aria into a drowsy century

For, the catchments of your love at initiation
Still trembles with the heavy saturation of fruity teats,

To nurture the Saharan springs
Of mankind's daily dreams.

And from the perennial flow, oh maternal songster,
Your heart-sprung daffodils shall crown

The yawning sky across the valleys of dread
Into flowering showers of your soul, in blue cycles...

Fair Play

Before you came, bright
And living with the bloom of life,
Others had come on different winds
From the uncertain world of winds,
And will still come like you, to live and leave.
So take a bit and leave a bit
From the bit that was left
For the bit that shall be taken.

I am a phoenix, changing as an amoebic cell under the strains of the world, ever changeless.

Before you came, I was the sun at dawn,
Always fresh and young, meeting others,
My only fuel for the flame,
And listen even now for a knock
In this eternal pilgrimage of meeting and parting.
So let's play not like players of a game,
But like visitors at a fair, coming to go.

When the game ends, God shall rise from the litter of old clothes to sing a song, changing the world, but changeless.

Dancer on The Edge of Life
(to the Memory of njinjoh abimne)

Over and beyond the shadow of life,
Death breeds kinship
From the plates of memory,
And the conscious heart
Weeps over neglected roses in the wind.

From shock of the cold beyond
We re count time in reluctant phrases,
With the enthusiasm of sleek tongues
Because the years have defined, finally,
The length of his fitful stride.

All his loves and hates
Gather in a pool of tears now,
Legions for the unfathomed heart in astral places.

He too felt the pulse of earth,
Groped the empty recesses

Of life, danced in siren halls,
But always on the edge of life,
Vagabond climber for the unknown hemisphere.

Who dares recall the chiding days
Of clamour and *revandications* and ridicule,
Girdled in oaths of denunciation?

Who dare now, cowards in pool of tears,
Harvesting kinship from scrubbed plates of memory?

He is not here anymore –
He has leapt over the frontier of memory,
Suddenly, and sailed into the bugling sphere
Of his quest, garbed in rainbow ribbons
Of his dissident faith, for venial seasons.

Sunset Helena

(*for jane anagho*)

She nestled at the trough of life
And wreathed beatitudes
In phoenix petals of passage.

And furrowed visages, black-veiled,
Tracked hooded dreams, strewn
In nostalgic hallucinations

Between the yawn and sneeze:
Pale remembrances of honey jests
Salute my orphaned hope, now.
Then grey chants
In toxic whiff, furl
My pious heart
Over the convulsed noon.

And my lyric, unprouded
In vacuum of death
Stoops to vacant dawns
In tinnitus inquisition.

Installers of Fear
for peter essoka, after 'Reflections,' 31-03-97

On the threshold of Easter,
scurried alleluias
tremble on alien mists of fission,
spewed from harassed breasts in pulpit feuds,
to usurp God.

But who, in pseudo Savimbi garb, and stalking the night,
still seeks to vindicate the breeder of a lake god's freckled
jargon,
attenuated over the National Station, that
ushers in, night after day, voodoo states of emergency
to cosmic ovation of the nightmare hour?

Who, Peter, counting the tombs of late, won't install fear
to derail the Mandellan wrath from earth-filled mouths

cuddled in the raped antecedents
of our psychic blot in hooded *dimabola*?

Or if, consider too, Oliver-Tamboed brains
smart from lethargic *Chococam*-makes
of a prodigal's micro-crumbs, grudged,
who can dare forestall the installation of fear
over the Mungo hearth stones, today?

What if cotton heads, scavenged

39

from cryptic bunkers onto marble pads
of Pelican glee are panting, panting
at midnight bellows
to force back the rush of kilned venom
divined in Rosenkreutz temples
of kilometric trots for Kribian blood banks
beyond radar altitudes?

They cringe in the orgasm of a bungled revelation,
wax-eared gallivant apostles
in blood temples,

and vow to again crucify the rising tide
across the Mungo, before this time tomorrow,
that rambles reflections in tortoise letters to Joshua
from the Midlands to the East,
and rolls Fako rock, minute by minute,
over the petering hilliness of dusk knowledge,
to witness what God has put asunder
over the Mungo bridge in *Obassinjom*.

So who, Peter, will not install fear
to whitewash the replica of Hiroshima, here,
refracted via Tienamen Square;
or such synonymous diplomatic abortions at Mini-Summits,
to spice blood to the prostrated leopard of Kinshasa,
or another ballistic crash from the ballotter's sneeze, who?

Obassinjom prophets have daily
conjured Ntarinkon emissaries
enlisting disciples on the eve of sunshine;
so who, Peter, alas, will not inaugurate terror
in the aftermath of cloakroom rituals,
to reign eternal in the despotic fealty
of Bokassa's Monrovia-in-Mombutu, forfeiting
the plebeian sunbath, as alleluia showers

40

still fill the tinnitus air with canister embraces?

You Can Smile, Brothers

When sun-plaited hills yawn in midnight
despondency
of the belching lord,
foster benefactors remember
nursery rhymes at cry-time.

Debunscha teats suddenly lapse too
in beggarly seasons,
fertilized by too much sweet talk from watery mouths,

As Mulafako limbs, chopped and coffined
in farting eighteen-wheels
and smelling the salty sands,
defy the plebeian wail, soon beating oars across the Suez.

But historical catchments and lighthouses
are intellectual antecedents and hardly
anchor next second's atomic rage of tumbling thrones
even with Delphian lenses, for the blundering mind.

So you can smile brothers,
you can still smile the cockcrow hour
in drumbeats of fattened *Mbaghelem*,
feasting in jazzy heaves, mournful.

Posted Memories
for schola

Purdue Dr., on a typical morning, in old Charleston
Wet in flakes,

Thinking:
A diary is a
Cruel crucifix
Fresh and withered,
Planted on vacant space,
Each man his allocated spot
In the vast emptiness of meaning,
Shedding tears
Along white, lonely streets;

A tourist in tears unshowing,
Scrubbing the plates of Boone Home
Shrouded in stunted oaks
That pegged slave shacks
For Baby Suggs, still straggling;

And then Sullivan's Island
With Ihuouma in the sun, watching
Her run soft white sand through delicate fingers
And the riotous waves from Wouri estuary
Conjure Francis Bebey blues in my ears;
Catching a strangled black wail gagged from civilised ears
Of America to revive cotton fields
Down South; the wet white sand
Hiding blood marks of history
When recalcitrant heartbeats blessed
The soil of America and washed horizons
To come, and I, a witness with pen and paper and a lens...

And Donald too, in sympathy
The following day, a crucifix on my mind, saying:
Hey, man! Shake a leg ... and stuff,
Shifting the stubborn, grumbling Chevy into gear.

But the spaces in my heart, heralded vacancy,
Are only the echo of his thoughts,

Robbed of a past
After which Timbuktu compensates
In yearly trips
From Federal stipends,
To search for meaning and a name, nodding,
And wean an estranged conscience.

And Ikena, the next baton-holder
In search of relics from Senegal
Now tearing through the house,
A lively storm
Up and down the staircase;
Or picking chess seeds with a healthy laugh
Over moody Kimberly,
Sisterly fighting back,
And summoning me, he, Ikena,
Ain't it cool man, how I lead my King?

Straddling walk in pizza fatigue
At lunch, besides Rivers Avenue
Giving back what was given me
Mechanically, to the ever marvelling acquaintances:
A smile, even from stiff conventional lips,
A wave or a nod,
Assembled as communal repertoire
To the initiate.

Or Lortie offering reprieves
With God's own voice,
Maternal and friendly, O ever so sweet,
And oiling another frantic day
That should go down on record,
Filling spaces and making life in Noelle dreadloacks,
On the snow-white lanes of
Rushing America,
To blot out the heart-breaking news from home...

The Heart in Exile
(for edouard bizimana)

I

The heart in exile
Weaves archetypes of salvation,
Treading needle heads
With Lenten lust

As the essence of Man
Blooms in tragic seasons:
He dares bubbling breakers of the Rubicon
To jericho Bujumbura Caligulas
In the tears fermented hour.

II

Yours is the footprint
Of Spring, Bizimana,
Retracing the bloodied contours.

You too palmed the fronds of
Apocalypse and from voodoo rituals
Across desert decades, fled.

Spray your balm then, rainbow
In my camped village; seed the hope
In your breast, for redneck destitutes in Muhinga.

Behind the hate-hooded sun,
Olive-girdled mermaids rehearse
Your riddles of diaspora

For, the heart in Exile
Dreams of salvation,
Schooled on needle heads.

Apocalypse

Beads of flame skirt
artesian dreams
under nebulous sky
when volleyed contentment
rolls on the laps of siren glee.

But a slash of cunning,
sudden at skygates,
heralds a prophet's apparition
and everywhere streams of tears
cart contemplative sins
into the hollow chambers of History.

Beads of flame,
God's redemptive crackers,
must shower sulphurs hearts
like resurrecting winds
along funereal footpaths
for my people to see the dawn
and the way ...

Epitaph

Shades of green
on a mask
of grey;
sun splashes
litter
dark, palmed streets, cuddled
in crimson fears;

and the passer-by, some time after,

laughs into a weeping moon:

Surely, these people
(Cupid-dazed in immemorial fantasy)
knew their destination
with mouthfuls
of parched corn;
they took the war cry
for Koubadji's[5] ditties,

and now
the evening tale
is sob for generations.

When the Bard Sings No More

I used to score goals from dreadlock hemispheres, they say;
now I concede shame at harlequin photo
opportunities of chop break-potters,
rubbing creams on nib-tip
for a once-upon-a-time shade of colour.
Mere cleavages of misty loves,
in snug chamber, harangued?
Or sugary revolutionary insanity from
conservative doublespeak forging new partnerships
begging for audience in Leftist tabloid columns
mimicking Che Guvera but toasting demise of Che Ngwa
Ghandi?
Ah! these tremulous presages, chemotherapeutic
against vengeance of Fako Gods,
before the whimper, my apology…

---

[5] nickname of a popular village hunter

Like the bookies I enticed,
prostitutes in the laps of fate; the Gods I tempted,
unblinking Nyamnkweh vanguards, long
before the speechy Natiramas conjured
ridiculous harmattan troughs
for plebeian comfort of a painted Deal
in *abola* Easters, year after year, remember?

With age I crawl unwise, baldied listener
to my own stray hooting, even senile
you may say, in gasping bardhood,
revoking the Pan-Africanist anthem
of my fiery days, most wanted then, and courted, weaving
Eve beatitudes to a blotted future, believed.
Remember what they used to say of me, and how:
he shall champion Matigari ma Njiruungi legions,
Ombudsman
against Etoudi dread, and navigate
Weka discourses for Alfred Nobel's *miyaka*!

Ah, the colour of dreams woven
in francaemiac trysts…

These tremulous presages, swollen dreams
gnawing at my soul,
memory of those Mbapelepe days
at centre stage of the Negritudinist rage, my apology.
Those who fanonised my song, hailed
Jerusalem in every verb, how were they to prophesy
the Wakiri jig, the surrogate exeunt, the watery-mouth
verbalism
now phrasing chichidodo verses in dust to dust,
preying on gory tragedy for lullabies of shame
at foul-fated foot of the Fako?

Franc Power

In my country today,
money can cook stones;
so they mint it from shit in nocturnal séances.

Such economics mechanics,
recruiting Malthus and eclipsing Keynes on a whiff of shit
after Camdessure's prescription, the pigmy's dread.

The people love to breed, not bleed;
but the ogre says, hearken only
the voice from above, amen!

The mutation of God, a miracle in francaemia,
and God the concept, defined
and equated in franc rhapsodies,

packaged in Calabar and sold at street corners in Yaoundé,
and the voice from the manger
remains fuddled in a rusted silver sheet.

Reply to Ted Jones

(after an evening)

Your sneaking steps
And nagging knocks
Have spermed the sandy membrane
Of our variegated chronicle;

Your timbral voice in polyphonic dreams
Recalls the black dirge
And lullaby of our rhythmic flow
Over greyed millennia
          - of the Middle Passage,

         - of Bismarck's Conference,
         - of Nkrumah's wail for Selaise's Mazrui,
         - of Camdessure's blood bank
Of a black paradise, spicing blood,

BECAUSE
Today, today of apocryphal sunrises
Nurtured from Machiavellian labs
In bunkered palaces of Africa's capitals
Against the day of glory;

BECAUSE
From cockpits of Kilimajaro-altitudes,
And from defruited Eden of Fako's laps
And along mined beaches-in-Bakassi
And mortgaged oil pumps of a Galian landlord,
Carting every mite into strongrooms
Of a French miser and along Zurich's lakeways;

Indeed, today of reigning Buthelezi fence-sitters
Breeding slaves in Savimbi mufti
(But scanning the darkened sky every hour
For armies of salvation jumbos),
To graze Mandella's earth in Tripoli's feudal rage
Because Sankaran tutelage is Zionist milk:

Your heavy and sad voice-in-Armstrong
Is the tear of unborn generations
Like Mandellan memory in rusted Victor Vorster:

For in today's Africa of tomorrow
And tomorrow's tomorrow,
The Africa of Timbuktu
Is a monstrous
Nightmare
In apologia.

Ode to a Poet Denied

Once his voice fed
Thunder bolts into incumbent
Conclaves; today
His laughter cracks the tar
On Buea's double lane,
The only road that *ends*.

The believer's plight to believe
Even as mushroom messiahs
Conjure God, darkly clad,
From phallic frenzy
For grey horizons, dripping red?

I, witness to seismic night after seismic
Night, know the blunt tongue
With inscrutable epithets of doom
That calcifies Tiko milk, (having chewed
Her teats in wanton rage, the returnee),
Skewers her dreams as ideological fodder,
Scares her kids with dreadlock whorls
And still brandishes the word without meaning.

Tragedy of believing humanity
In a petering universe, still nodding
To verbal rot, dazed by the incessant rape
Of the mind, because the living God has been murdered
And resurrected as a concept
Now in the Synod or at Bishop's House;
And the don in high credentials rushes after Party silver
While the once-upon-a-time Seer
Denies his own Frankenstein monstrosities, shivering.

African Millennium Jive

In panic-wrecked nights of moribund catechisms
Savimbi tongues have enacted Basque iniquities
In Twarek shrines of Monrovia's Deathlords, since
Seminal gardens must bud gestapo acolytes
Hurling Alfred Nobel in Mogadishu's back streets.

New Deal gawkers in Ujamaa deserts, have
Auctioned Eké emporia in Dow Jones arithmetic,
And the sulphurous horizons in Katanga,
Spit manna in *abola* seasons, meaning rain.

Ostentatious *akunyams*-in-barratry,
Pocketing plebeian sweat in Judas-chants,
Have planted ballot boxes in muttering households,
Proclaiming dehydrated goodwill in baton love.

Midnight blood then recoils from burdened loins,
Wasted for Moloisean decades of shanty hope;

Grim fantasy then grows on the brows of night
As grand-standed rhythms of death
Assume champagne poses in marble places,

As no one dares fathom the land's own tomb
In aftertime of the Africanna vacuum;
And sharpen the spear of battle,
From turbulent breast
To appease the wail of Ethiopia, echoing the ages.

Nemesis

Nothing but fear
gnawing my heart, a shuddering thought,
the crunching of bones,
licking of blood
and the collapsed vision;

as we enthrone misery
in denial,
ensure new histories
and new geographies
and the incessant crunching of bones
between night and day
when nothing is said and nothing is done
because the invisible hand seals the lips,
twists vision,
and plastic smiles
spell our new history without contours.

Dangling Horizons

Those who dine from swings
in Kribi or Down Beach
see paradise in their laps,
manna for the chosen few,
such double-mouth monsters;
dream-chunks of the fat Italian chef
dipped in Mouton Cadet
and direct debited to a Swiss strongroom.

Crimson showers from the skyline
replicated in a daze of epicurean patriotism
of chop broke potters,
which they take for anniversary confetti:

forever blind to the Bakingili dread
that too much of love and hatred
would trigger, when swinging lusts
substitute the dangling horizons
and cue in wail on deceit.

In the Shadow of My Country

There is peace,
away
from the crowd
and god's face shines
in the dark, ever;

I trail the kite for guide
along uncharted space
where a lily on tombstone
marks decades of a heavy tale,

as the lintel of time
toys my name,
excavating the king's earth-filled mouths.

Prophet Meka

Meka was his own prophetic victim,
his land and his sons and the archetypal future—
devalued collaterals for a toy.

The *boucarie* that conspired against his raw manhood
and the snarling sun of his ancestors
became fangs of God's white man.

When I followed his voice, it led to a fallowed trail in the brain
at the end of which, in futuristic whorls
was a monument on which was grafted

two verses, a broken rainbow:
A nous la Patrie, and in perfect translation,
Ah, why am I here!

Oracle of Tears

At midnight of the divining return,
The gong of dark
With generations in scale,
Bruises the womb-lobes
In a priestal dirge;

And labouring mothers again
Pause in unending trance at passage-gate;

And the owl again
Hoots the cataclysmic hour at hand;

And the anxious *mekwire*[6]
Sees only a dawn of convulsions
Wrapped in vague whites, ahead.

---

[6] Traditional midwife in Pinyin